GHOST CHILD OF THE ATALANTA BLOOM

Praise for Ghost Child of the Atalanta Bloom

"Explosive, turbulent, haunting, magnetic, Rebecca Aronson's *Ghost Child of the Atalanta Bloom* begins with a girl who sets a field on fire, an apt metaphor for poems that are themselves fiery. Mortality and death undergird Aronson's fantastical visions, where a child becomes a seagull, a woman turns tarantula, and a house threatens to fill with blood. Fierce vulnerability and brutality excite the perceptions of the ill and the grief-stricken, the child and the new mother who claims: 'With teeth I guard the home, and with breathing.' Details are vaulted to life, wild with electricity—from a canoe to a pearl to a bobbin, 'even the grass / could be an engine of desire.' An acute and visceral brightness—an aliveness—reaches under the eyelids, floating the reader across startling landscapes and dreamscapes, from Pompeii to Jersey City. I could stare all day at the riot of gasping colors, enthralled by Aronson's poems and her 'Ravenous god of little things.'"

—Hadara Bar-Nadav, judge of the 2016 Orison Poetry Prize

"The poems in Rebecca Aronson's collection achieve a longed-for but near-impossible mark—they change the very shape and length of the momentary to make time last longer. How does the present, each held breath, bloom and stretch and become an ever-ness, a sustained cherishing? This poet infuses more life into a line than almost any of her peers. This book belongs in a canon with the works of Brigit Pegeen Kelly, Naomi Shihab Nye, James Richardson, and Rita Dove—we have always needed new paths into that deep, attentive, porous and mindful way of being that only poetry can offer. Aronson's is a new route into our oldest and most familiar paradoxes and mysteries, those of love, beauty, connection, (im)materiality and consciousness. Nobody but Rebecca Aronson turns a reality inside out just by the way she looks at it, the way she listens, to reveal ever deeper colors and music than we could have suspected were all around us, and in us."

—Brenda Shaughnessy

GHOST CHILD OF THE ATALANTA BLOOM

poems by Rebecca Aronson

ORISON BOOKS

Orison Books
PO Box 8385
Asheville, NC 28814
www.orisonbooks.com

ISBN 978-0-9964397-0-1

Distributed to the trade by Itasca Books
1 (800) 901-3480 / orders@itascabooks.com
www.itascabooks.com

Manufactured in the U.S.A.

ORISON
BOOKS

Table of Contents

I.

II.

III.

Acknowledgments

Thank you to the editors of the journals in which the following poems have appeared (sometimes in somewhat different versions or with different titles):

Adobe Walls: "Flood, Postscript" & "Impact"
American Poetry Journal: "Dream 1" (formerly "Yellow Dream"), "Dream 2" (formerly "Green Dream") & "Parking Lot, Pre-Dawn"
Catch Up: "Dinner Party" (formerly "Sequence")
Cutbank: "While I Breathless" & "Telescope"
The Freeman: "Wish"
I-70 Review: "My Father Robs an Etruscan Grave," "The Museum of Inattention," "Starship," "Late Elegy with Eyeshadow," & "Overgrowth"
Manifest West: Serenity and Severity (*Volume 5, Manifest West Series Anthology*): "The First Act," "Los Alamos Fire," & "Home"
MARY: A Journal of New Writing: "Self Portrait with Uterine Fibroids" & "Erosion"
Mas Tequila Review: "Fire Season" (formerly "Burn Chronicle")
Panoplyzine: "Shadow"
The Paris-American: "I Was the Girl Who Set the Field on Fire"
Pilgrimage: "North-Going Phantoms"
Prairie Schooner: "Bat & Watchers" (formerly "Bat") & "World"
Quarterly West: "Buried City"
Reservoir: "In the Underground Museum Called Infinity"
Rose Red Review: "Flood"
Stealing Time: "Walking to School" (formerly "Memory")

"Bat & Watchers" and "World" were the 2010 winners of the *Prairie Schooner* Strousse Award.

So many thanks to the people who helped this book along the way. In particular, thank you to the tremendously talented and hilarious Erin Adair-Hodges for lending her laser beam eyes and good brain, for her unflagging willingness to read the whole thing yet again, and for collaboration, commiseration, and happy hour. Also to Nancy Mayer, for her many rounds of manuscript reading and always right-on-the-money observations and questions, and for her special brand of wry cheerleading. I am forever grateful also to my traveling writing group who helped so much with early versions of this book—Emmy Pérez, Oody Petty, Patricia Machmiller, and Renata Treitel—and whose conversation, support, and friendship have been so important to me over all these years. Thank you to James Arthur for thoughtful critique; to Richard Greenfield for warm encouragement and such helpful comments, and for pinning down the "lyric escape pod"; Colrain crew for being there; Brenda Shaughnessy for her kindness and generosity and for her own work, forever; the amazing Hadara Bar-Nadav for choosing this book and helping it into the world; and super-editor Luke Hankins and Orison Books for attention to detail, thoughtful reading, and taking such care with my book. And to Tim and Levi, my heart.

I.

I Was the Girl Who Set the Field on Fire

Someone had left a can of lighter fluid
beside the trash cans.
There were plastic chairs,
womanly with their smooth white arms,
dry grass harrowing ankles
and small yellow moths drifting
among tasseled heads.
When she spun, the world tilted and blurred
to a golden rush.
Drops flew from the red can,
became the throng of this new hour,
stung and swarmed her limbs
lightly buzzing a song
she knew.
She lit the single match
filched from its watch house
above the mantel—
the rough cap
flaring into sunburst—
the world a slingshot
flinging loose its load
of unfixed colors.
The pitch transformed
into ripples
that spread to flaming trails, concentric
and growing wider around this girl
held in the thrall of her own knack.

My Father Robs an Etruscan Grave

It was the kind of fever in which want burns.
The tomb site exposed,
ground bleeding its ripe scent
into the buzzing ribbon of darkened sky—
a loose cover under which I moved
between small bright lights set close,
my hands busy among afterlife's
few luxuries: a shard of pot
that once held grain, a tiny cup,
armies of clay nails.

I took them: to touch
the hardened, indiscernible whorls
of two-thousand-year-old fingerprints seared
into molecules of crumbling clay,
the breath in my throat rushing out
like bats, those same wings
gone skimming the night winds now as then.

Buried City

We were stronger than oxen, raised on sweet
water and the musky flesh of clean-shot
beasts. The clear sky was a flickering vault.

At times the ground staggered under our feet.
We thought it volatile and hungry.
We carved broad halls with smooth stone benches

flush to walls. We seldom drew together,
preferred instead our solitary lives. One to a home,
one to a bed, and one wide bowl to fill.

When the skies suddenly closed, stonemasons
lifting mallets and chisels stilled; the town sweeper
lay down next to his broom and slept.

This is how they found us, frozen in mud casts,
our bodies dissolved down to bone and cloth.
No one who saw the imprints would know

we were the ones who named the world. Hallowed
the mountain which formed us, yes, but forgot
the hungry dirt that would someday call us back.

The Museum of Inattention

Here is a room of forgotten sweaters,
the orange silk scarf left at the Vancouver airport,
single gloves leaping from pockets, some of them
clutching crumpled bills. Here is a ballroom,
its elegant display of expired parking meters
shimmering under a dome of shooting stars.

The door I almost missed was so blue
my feet fell toward it and I was in,
like stepping into a puddle of sky.
I must have slept on the tram to the upper levels.
Here is me, turning away just as the baby
reaches my legs on his first room crossing.

I don't recall what floor this is.
This wing is a maze of classrooms,
each with a foggy window in an unmarked door
blank as a centaur's blind eye.

Here is the roof garden.
There I am shaking sand free from a beach towel—
and there is the birthday watch with its delicate shining strap
flying loose from the frame of my noticing.

Here is the bed I turned from my love in.
A cluster of words, the flock of ears they fled from.
Here are two throbbing packets of lost crushes—
the unrequited ones rudely knocking each other's edges,
the ones I never knew existed floating
like cartoon ghosts through cartoon walls.

The exit is invisible. Walk past it
and you'll find yourself where you usually go
at this same time on a different day.

Town

Maybe I thought I was invisible,
the town's one ghost, in my imaginary den.

Maybe I believed that my special power
was to disappear through my own front door,

leave a space as blank as the line next to church
on the real estate questionnaire.

I moved through the house at night,
undressing, thinking only of a glass of water

or the numeracy of shadows
until I came home late and saw

the upstairs hallway lit open, each room's
contents vague in the hall light's glow,

the bed with its clotted sheets, my favorite dress
sprawled on a chair, the mirror

on the closet door reflecting everything.
Everyone walked in the weedy roads.

Maybe I thought that I couldn't be seen
because I knew I wouldn't stay.

Road Runner

I am burning
    in my bed, burning
        in the dry air while
    silt settles
on my eyelids and curled tongue.
    I made this tinderbox
        my favorite dream,
    bid it into existence,
thinking of red clay
    until I found it
        under my fingernails.
    All those years of sighing over postcards
of carnivorous birds,
    their beaks cocked
        at jaunty angles,
    until I dug this dry plot
to live inside, these stunted
    tomatoes struggling among the cosmos
        and calendula.
    I might have built myself, too,
from sticks and mud,
    little adobe body
        with calavera face.
    The mountains run their color-show
until they disappear into smoke
    which eats the sky then rains
        only dust and hail. Moths emerge
    ravenous, beating
powdery wings across my dry cheeks.
    I wake parched,
        lightning far away.

The First Act

There's wildfire
shearing the mountain,

leaving a smear of ash for a coat, cindering
knots of trees and abandoned hides.

What's left is a scorched shell so brittle
seedlings will storm through the surface.

From down here it will seem a riot of green gems
has erupted, a sleek new skin

to mask the burning city
which hovers at the periphery of sleep

coveting breath. We choose our dangers.
This high desert, piñons torchy

among parched understory, electrical sky,
radioactive remnants simmering in red rock,
this gun with its invisible trigger.

North-Going Phantoms

Moth season. Insect dust
leaves trails on our arms and cheeks

as we walk in the darkened yard.
In the lightning bush alive with small worlds

window-pane wings flash and glaze.
The neighbors' cats make daring rooftop leaps.

Summer wanes after sunset, but only a little.
This could be some far planet of the mind

where we lost our way a long time back,
night rising and sinking in lapping wavelets.

Either way, this falling apart could turn out just fine.
I am letting the harness of bad news—

human news—loosen and tumble away
so as not to end each day in anxious

fervor. The garage roof is old and caved
where rain tore it open, but the cats glide

from station to station, lean silhouettes
pattering nimbly among the ruins.

Overgrowth

When she lost the yard I knew
        a change had come.
In the kitchen were sealed boxes
        whose every crease was sharp
as a shiny knife. An illusion.
        The blade would only gum the bread and tomatoes
dully. Where the back gate used to hinge,
        a Rose of Sharon
crochets itself over slats.
        The handle seals us in
or out and something nests now
        as the days' disorder deepens in us.
From the parapet a faint shrieking, someone
        in need of rescue or the dusk frenzy of bats
hungry for the ordinary irritations
        of our waking.
Here is the story
        as if chronology were the main matter:
before the climbing vine the house
        shone in every kind of light
but now it's better,
        secret as a buried ladle.

Late Elegy with Eye Shadow

She died twenty years ago,
hadn't done her face
for the decade of her slow decline

from cocktail dresses and decorative wigs
to hospital gowns, blunt nails chipped
and bare. Her jewelry is divided now, smoldering

in boxes, my sister's cache of gold and gems,
my tangle of outsized butterfly pins with mock-jewel eyes,
an accidental diamond

lost in the snaky rubble of rhinestones.
There must be biological hazards
in a thirty-year-old stick of makeup,

but I smear it on because in the pictures
her eyes and mine, my father's
and even my son's surprising blue, are duplicates

in only passingly similar faces.
She would blend the thick lines
into her creped lids, add Cleopatra wings

and an orange bow mouth, spray L'Air du Temps
into cleavage and rub the pulse points
of her wrists, the lobes of her ears,

slip her tiny feet into high, pinched heels
and take hold of the first steady arm offered.
When she died I wanted her to be dressed

for the city, shimmery sheath and matching oversize bag,
not bleached in hospital whites,
her teased red beehive cropped into a pale skullcap.

She entered the ground
as if tucked in a doll bed, her padded coffin cozy,
though the funeral day was bitter and wheezing

and the limo ride lonely
without her gloved hand clutching my arm
to direct my wandering attention

to all the world's derelict theaters and ruined
supper clubs, that once-familiar drive,
requiem to the glories of Jersey City.

Tea Cup

The boy on her lap eclipses her
beneath the span of his legs
which have come to rest

somewhere on the carpet
below the frame.
She is a tiny landscape,

the tremendous peak of her hair,
her Matterhorn, rising in the bold distance.
He is the new development

with his shining modern eyes
and elaborate gears, yet untested,
destined for technical difficulties.

She is burnished—a low glow
emanating from the golden threads
of her dress, her imperial heels—

and beaming in the photograph
though she may already know
how unsteady this curl-headed boy

will be on his outsized feet.
She will not raise him.
She has raised herself

to her full height and taken the boy
by his already substantial arm;
they will walk as far as the garden path

stopping to examine the petals
of each of the chestnut roses
she plants wherever she has lived

and which are blooming still
on the delicate porcelain tea cup
the boy did not take from her last house.

Turbulence

The small plane dropped—lurch of gut into clouds—
and recovered, as we each unpaled, gasping,

and the window settled its blurred view.
I fear leaving that world now. Down there,

where compass-circles are etched
inside green-gray checkerboard fields

and streaks of roads and riverbeds are chalky,
drought-dry, water towers winking

into sun-glare and dust rings over the town
where red mountains shade my son

as he hums in the yard's blue light, pressing
his small fingers together, trying

to crack the air with his clear snap.

II.

Starship

All the yard's insects come out.
This hour's shadow is a sinking ship.
Children devising deaths
bicker, my boy and his friend,
litter the ground with the delicate hinges
of legs and lost wings, translucent
discs, a periphery
of hobbling escapes.
The boys are ambassadors of a future
swampy with despoilment, fathomless, rabid
for yogurt tubes and joyful
over a new species of grasshopper
that can, they say, live
limbless and mudded, willing
to eat the tiny bruised petals
pinched from the leggy basil just now
gone to flower.

Impact

I wished the birds into their little houses and they flew in, built nests, left pale doll heads and small monocles among the wiry twigs and plucked hairs. I willed the porch cat tame and it purred for a bowl of milk and led wobble-legged kittens to the front mat, where they grew wings and spurted fire from pink mouths. Here the tree I climbed as a child was cindered by lightning. I floated the yard anchorless, skimming peony blooms from their glossy bushes. Up drifted the ponds and down the clouds. I flew and was as tall as a leaf. I asked for the world to be restored and through the window the charred stump listed and the wind tugged at the hems of stones and the ocean that once was here pushed off from its now faraway shores.

Home

I wake blind in a striped cell.
I wake from a hot, black sleep
to find the sun, a man-hole cover,
stomped down tight. I move through a field
of dry stalks rustling a reedy cantata,
woodwind in hollow sands, the music
of shrew and ragweed.
I came here for a mountain.
I came here for a poet. I came here
for something I imagined about horses.
I fell into a snake hole that held me.
When the rains came I was released
as high tide releases driftwood from the shoreline.

Some come to the desert to plant gardens;
some come to bury the dead
in shallow ditches. Some to disappear,
to turn themselves into Century plants,
biding time. I know a woman
who turned tarantula.
Her night face is a painted skull.
She climbs out of her cavern
into the dark cover of cicada song, into cloud cover
or snow pack, from a hole the wind carved.
My house is the color of dried blood.
When it rains, the walk runs red
and I am always
hoping for rain.

Los Alamos Fire

The city held its breath.
That is, we in the city held our breath.

The dog-walkers tugged leashes to a slow stroll
while dogs panted for speed.

The neighbors with their cream skin and kewpie eyes
reached for one another in the morning light.

The woman with a once-dark braid
gave stern instructions to her damaged son.

We simmered together with sore lungs and waited.
The air became visible

and settled around us seared particles
of forests. As odor contains remnants

of its object, my head aches with crumbled monuments
and spoiled crops, with the charred bodies of deer and wood
mice,

radioactive ash the burning ground releases.
No one has said a grave is not a grave

when the buried thing still lives.
No one will say it's time to leave.

Parking Lot, Pre-Dawn

The only light this hour
a sheen of crisp ice refracting
from last week's snow piles; a woman

steps onto crushed gravel, her hips
barely brushing the grills of cars
as she drifts with a wobble

from one to the next, her gloved hand
leaving a three-pronged trail
along the icy metal.

Watching from a window above, I imagine
the scuff of fabric on frost,

the almost palpable almost-sound,
a vibration making its way to me
until the thread is broken

by the helix of an alarm.
She stops. Then
as all of the proximal dogs weigh in

and the weak winter sun begins its ascent
she sheds a pale scarf like a loose feather
before stepping toward the door

and, trailing the wings of her red coat,
plunges into the brief brightening there.

Make No Little Plans

I used to dare myself to feats of danger:
to wear the black stilettos from my sister's closet
to the party, to walk in without falling.
To use a dictionary to flirt in Greek
with strangers leaving discos.
I held packets of fire in my palms,

offering my burning truths to anyone.
At seven my son pats my hand and coaxes me
onto the Ferris wheel, conquering
our fear of heights. At the top
we will the seat motionless in the gusty wind,
invent a song in which all of the words are thunder.

We practice the same two steps: say the thing
you want to do, then do the thing you've said.
Reward yourself with fried dough and a circus act
in which a dozen riders on small bikes
roar at one another from high platforms,
a hair's breadth between them,
a tangled knot the wheels only just slip.

Walking to School
For LRA

The broken-loose dog caught scent and dove
for the cluster of puffed hens scattering fast
to hedges and railings; five escaped,
barely and not unscathed. The sixth
became a spent balloon deflating quickly. I wonder
how you'll remember this morning's walk.
That I dropped your hand and took off
calling after the run-away, breathlessly and too late,
or the collapsed chicken twitching slightly
before going still in the empty street?
No blood, just plumage drifting like blown leaves.
Nobody noticed you at first, one foot then another
edging to the sight of that first death.

Charm

Ravenous god of little things,
holder of hairpins in floor cracks,

of a long-lost emerald-eyed glass dog,
keeping them all for your own mean gems,

what luck you must have offered the rough grass
when, in a lawn, a door

slipped open; objects tumbled
into your inestimable mouth

to stick between your ribs.
They gather companions and are themselves

worlds inhabited by worlds,
and somewhere, fixed to that dog's golden collar,

a seed pearl in which
a kite string unceasingly unwinds.

World

In a woods, I find a wide carpet of bluebells
and the sky just visible through
a lattice of leaves; the air, fine
sheen on dampening sleeves. I am made clean,
porcelain and tulle, skimming the bright ground.
The photograph is a surprise, then, this girl
lumped in wool, skin the color of clay,
a post sunk in a swamp of startling blue.
Forgive me my vanities. I had thought
I could be made a mirror.

~

In the pond
a large toad,
its shining throat
catching light—
a signal
one might think
mistakenly.

~

Here I am, in this small wooded tableau,
under the weather, the mantle, singing
off my mudded boots.

~

One eye is on an oak tree
from where a low hoot—
and one is shut tight
to keep out the dark.

~

Fearsome is a field where a herd approaches
all lowing some with horns and drifting close
they of the curious great orbs blinking
with sweet menace or dumb beneficence
who will lope ever faster to keep pace.

~

I had intended once to know these things.
Particulars of light, velocities
and wing spans. The least characteristics
of green-spored lepiota.

~

Recall the blinding passage the ice made.
Treetops bowed to the road, shivering
a rain of wreck and thunder between rests
in which the only light was shine. Breath
held and blood halted in veins. Weather
made this over, cast this kindred of spells
that only broke when all else fell to ruin.

~

I thought I could be made a mirror.
Bright ground which held me to it, filigree
resurfacing greenly. I am solid
as any stump nursing old wounds under
a pinkish sky. Just there, the tallest tree
standing, cracked through to the taproot, one branch
leafing. The floor a heaven of mushrooms.

Dominion

All day
barns flash by
crisp as accordions,
dove wings
etching
frail
gills into
hot sky.
Inland,
Jesuits
knot bells,
languid
moonscape echo of
Nebraska dunes.
Onwards.
Pie Town serves
quince and
rhubarb all
summer.
Today
unveils
wonder: rainless flowering,
xeric shrub lands,
yellow sky hovering, a storm
zone.

Perimeter

I was born on the outer edge of my birth day,
forehead rumpled as linen.
Existence is a mystery, they say,

the enigma of one's own left
wrist, how it aches before stormy weather,
how the metal plate

must have been overtaken by now,
like the tree that enfolded the bicycle
left so long leaning.

The doctor said the screws would slowly
unscrew themselves right out of the thin fabric
of the arm—who knows if already the loosening is underway,

indecipherable as so many of the body's events,
the cancers colonizing my father's liver
and the lining of my mother's bladder—

the first known and measured,
inexorable, the second appearing overnight
like mushrooms after rain, little outcrops

pluckable and persistent—
all of which indicates the body does not guard
itself so well, but also that it does:

take me, for example, on my back in the grass
milled over by countless bacteria, billions
I presume, and yet my borders hold.

In the Deep

Here is a mother in the park,
her boy milky with noon-day sun,

a plum, floating in the sweet syrup
of his own dampened shirt.

His sleeping mouth refuses
even a drop of the water

that has pulled itself forward
from his cup's orange-lit rim

to hover and crash minutely
onto the dry sill of his lip.

What he held of the world
he has released, the green ball

now lost somewhere
back before the last corner.

His sleep and her fear
are cavernous expanses

both will dive from
keeping the edges always in sight.

Dog

You moan in your sleep, grinding the night down
to a bare leash that would snap
at the lightest tug. You are dreaming your freedom
in tight circles which widen
a hog's hair at a time, breadth
of breath that shimmies into the broad sky
and is gone. Poof. Who
doesn't long to disappear
like a body into a hole, a magic-show
pigeon, a margarita? Worry wakes you
seven times and seven times you circle,
excavating a bare path in the dense cover
of your bed. There is safety
in the hours of darkness, the air salty
as a long-buried bone. Sleep is thunderheads
just past the mountain. You sense a storm
panting on the horizon, your nose wet
with want; though it is heading your way
there is no knowing
if it will stay on course
or veer like a fox, the path foiled, far
from the sure lock of your hunger.

Bat and Watchers

Once I was a pearl in a lobe, oblong
and exuding subtle phosphorescence.

Say you knew me then, your tongue
on the cold jewel of me.

I was a bobbin wound tight,

all recoil and little give. Or you might have known me
best as a belled collar, a bird-alarm,

broadcasting my ward's intent. How I wished
to be a helicopter, swift helix

unanchored, everything mine but for gravity…

~

There was a cave at dusk where we waited:

bats hurtling into the mussel-shell sky.
In quick disorder, they spearheaded lampposts

where insects nightly met, halo
of moonlight blurring wings to soft slurries.

The night was clear and quick and full. It ran us
the long course, garbled, grateful

as nests. At the bar everyone talked
of leaving but no one left. What we drank

was sweet, venom-like, but didn't kill us.
The crowd murmured and chirped in surges.

We moved by blind touch, mapping as we met.

We missed our bodies slipping back through dawn.

~

What is sound to the open air or smell
to the salted sea? The clouds rebuff all

shrill calls. Kept thus safe, we dive.
Plunder the light, plunder the bulbs' bounty,

the open sky all ripe and buzzing. Full
as banquet boards we swarm down so weighted

it is a wonder the walls will hold us.

~

What was I once? Caved, kept, a modest shock.
Star of film and dream. Someone's night of slate

and sweat. Foreshadow and plot twist, intent
on entanglement, I'd dart and scurry.

~

You of the midnight startle. In the floor boards
where no entrance shows. Stairwell, woodpile. Glint

on the drab wall where once a mirror hung.
On sleeping lips, a twitch that says you've been here.

I find you, sudden
staccato flutter, waking's blur, cornered,

a bracket of dark matter glossy and gone.

Dream Dictionary Abecedarian

All night I dream of mother,
bent "C" on her bed
calling. *We are late*, she says,

despite this visit unannounced, unplanned.
Except dying, what so sidelines us?
Forget those watching it unwind. My mother

grips her life and my hand and I see
how this dream unspools me.
I am not crying, I tell my tears.

Jumped awake by the alarm, my face a pond,
koi and water-walkers busy below and above,
limned surface reflecting clouds where I am

mired among their bulky shapes. I'm dreaming again,
no doubt, and there are children floating,
Ophelia-like, but only faking; they laugh,

pose and my anxiety recedes.
Quietly, a forest has appeared around me.
Right now I am fitting fragments of tiny eggs

slowly back together. Weeds
tentacle my legs, fingers of slippery grass slide
under my body where I am stretched out

viewing that pond, which beckons me
with its water-arms. I am the spot—
x-marked, but out of reach. My glasses

yellow the world to an old photograph, a road
zigzagging straight out of the frame.

In the Underground Museum Called Infinity

Bats were here and something that never ate
the bones. Piles of tibia and fibula,
little forks for wishing,
not arranged yet into anything.
Here could be a spray of feathers
to frame a ribcage, itself an arbor
of gristle. Lovely
bridges over interlaced channels
knit archipelagos
from light.

Or have I mistaken daytime
for pretty vision? Beyond the anteroom
there is likely no need for looking.

                ~

In the ice wing, nothing can be reached.
The thick walls waver and distort their contents—
is that a lung in the south corner,
above the window seat? The air is dense,
a crystalline slurry.

But this is the wrong view.
The ice wing is a dream of perfect beauty—
all shine and surface and slide.
As in a petrified forest, every shape
was something else. A witch's hat,
a quarantine cage, a café.
Only the railings are not slick. They reach for you,
shy tentacled creatures
in the ocean shallows. Hello
from beneath. Hello.

III.

Thinking About Cells in the Undersea Room at the Aquarium

Fish eye fogged and unblinking, I too am filled
with unseeing. The world half invisible,

half inaudible.
Flashes of color hover and fin

above rocky outcrops pressing the known limits
of spectacle; here on dry land I am deceived

by shades and shapes. But there are worlds of blue
that have nothing to do with sky.

Tentacle, polyp, garden of subterranean blossoming.
Luminescent fragments deep in forests

resembling doll arms. Underworld, I am lost
long before any cavernous plummet unfoots me.

X-rays are of scant use. The inner vision needed
is micro or necro-, sectioned tissue-thin slices

on a glass slide, magnified to reveal a blown-open nimbus
of gorgeous particulate, which, if pooled, might tumble

against its own edges, discover architecture, become
constructed, gluey, sentient.

Shadow

At first light she will map
the contours of his leg

faintly, tiny hairs rising under her touch
in a reversed domino effect,

one after another standing
as her hand's shadow passes,

as a bird steers its dark likeness
above a damp and rippling field

courting the moment of descent.

Dream 1

There was a thin string I pulled with my teeth
to unzip you. You on the deck gasping,
water puddled where you lay. The bright sun.
When we kissed it was teeth that met, then tongues.
Inside, a red blanket hung over the window,
you on the bed, glowing. You the salt
I come into the world to taste. Shy, I graze
your hands and neck. *Show me the way from here.*
In the back garden yellow squash grown huge
under their broad leaves. Little blossoms still
arriving. Cherry tomatoes ripe on the vine.

Dream 2

There's a leaf from your hair you have offered
to me. I will mouth it delicately
from your palm, a hungry colt.
We are dancing as we used to, eyes locked
while our bodies float in the music's room.
I have fallen into sound. There will be
no sleep for me—consumed by your presence
on the fold-out sofa. Dry fronds rattle
the patio doors all night. We wake
to footprints in the snow there, spreading fast
in the wet melt. A bobcat, I told you,
hopeful. It's a long time before snow again
and the dance, at last, is in a renovated theater.
A leaf drifting between plush seats for anyone
to notice, but you were the only one.

Oyster Bar

You are thinking
this is a dream, but the child
ran to the edge of the pier

and spoke to the sea lions
as if they were his own brothers.

The ocean was intercom static,
a wedge of lemon.
The child became a seagull

worrying trinkets from wet sand.
The beach behind us
became a lost dog, its soggy smell

pleading for scraps. Dazed in the hazy sun,
we woke sunk in careful sarcophagi,

lacquered with tiny crab legs,
feet seaweed shrouded, the sanctified day
trumpeting color across the horizon,

a reason and a reason and a reason for joy.

Telescope

Through the glass brought close—wavelets frothing—
white under a white sky—late day shine
late ache pulling all the strings homeward

on the beach a sea lion—young, alone—
we worry of course—motherless child—
a voice calling would be lost in wind,
salt-fogged windows obscuring vision

shrimp boats and small heads, tilting under
resurface—far later and away—
sated, fish in the bellies of both.

Erosion

What am I to sand? Flea and a bother.
Some brotherless mud hen brooding for dusk.
These long nights start early. Sun pillaring
cloudbanks. Watch. It'll stripe out before long.
Go crazy with color the way it does.

What in the sea will say what it wants—
as a child collecting sand dollars—
each wave making a swift grab, *this* and *this*.
So these birds died on the shore or under
the cold wash—there they are, looking all wrong.

Horizon is an ever moving thing—
No, you'd say, it's fixed just there, only clouds
reconfigure perception. I blink to clear my vision, wishing:
Presto. But the birds are not re-flying. They're still still.
The sand taking of them such little sips.

Dinner Party

Before the minute hand moved forward
other signals arrived, musical

in their way. In their midst, a kind of frenzy,
insect-like and radial; apparently

a quiet night revolts in such sonic
correspondences. In the meantime, talk:

our words were saucy and slightly blurred, not
by the wine or the late, long dinner, not

by the modicum of hydroponic
weed or the wailing, orchestral starshine,

not by the impossibility of
saying just what we mean, though I give you

that those conditions all apply.
We are not wires

crossed too closely, making intimate sparks inside
the hard shell of a narrow container

until combustion melds us completely.
Maybe we are a wing and a wing

these nights, a cricket
sawing a song from its one whole body.

White Room, Clear Morning

Between breaths time seems glacial, episodes
of upheaval and perfect stillness. We wake

inside the sheet's sunny corona,
a white eye which reflects us

back into ourselves. Carry the moment
forward and it becomes equally wish

and worry-stone, rubbed smooth against itself.
Who are we to ask so much of bodies,

those simple thugs which knock and grab, yearning
for such chronic, satisfying likeness?

Peril

When you ask as you move your lips along
my arm tasting where I am I say *I'm here right
here* and this means I am pulling
my self down into my body again
from where it has drifted—though I do try
to watch—past the periphery. I am
forever slipping away unnoticed.

This is true: desire is peril. I want.
I want. I bay at the door of wanting.
The trouble is the door—it slides from side
to side, it goes incognito or a-
way. Unlike me; there I am, knocking, see,
in the wrong place, pulling the dresser's knob
for instance and waiting to be let in.

Flood

And just as before the bridge,
topsoiled water
is sweeping twig cities
free from their scaffolds,
mud-made walls debone
themselves
into untrackable wakes
which eddy and spit brief nests
onto the surface
where they swirl and foam,
looking from here like small hands
cupping air.

Flood, Postscript

River-troll, I am asking
where on the dry banks
should a girl lie? Where
have the heads of children
softened the brittle reeds
for nesting? And where
will a roving eye reap
the richest yield?
My finger works the mud,
questioning. If stick and worm
will not equal one another,
which is a bird's first necessity?
I am only asking. Here is the line
where water came to drink the roots in.
Call it a drowning. Here the rocks
followed as if magnetized.
Silly, I know the water doesn't
thirst. There's nothing there but molecules
gone riotous with gravity; surely
a kind of rapture
to dissolve what you touch
as you race past
in the like company
of countless others.

Luminosity and Other Measurements

After, the floor still flooded
with sunlight something small enough
could drown in. Single-celled bodies
or variable stars, those
pulsing a million years past the fact.
All that wasted time. Once
when the phone was off the hook for hours
I felt like that. Always there are dust mites
shoring up the linens. A little bit
of everyone who rested here.

~

Under the porch light
white moths throw themselves
against the torn screen in rhythmic volleys.
Ornamental clouds drop rain
that dries up before it hits earth.
Lightning season
and everything is always flashing.
We wake to find moths on every surface,
thousands. Before dawn we have killed them all.

~

In summer I drove from heat to hail, a sudden storm that burst
three tires, rubber ribbons spooling out. Such luck, such radiant
air   shimmering
up from black asphalt, a ghost

of frozen rain. There was a tour I missed with obligatory stops
        for shopping.
I waited years
to look for a clay pot like the ones I might have seen,
        but by then

it was hard to remember wanting one.

~

At the first melt I wreck my shoes with mud,
deliberate in careless walking. Sea shells
surface in paved lots, as if an ocean
washed through in the night. Soon sounds
will return, like the green shoots
I hope survive the last frost. Unhinged
by light, the houses waver
and everyone sighs from open windows.
I am returned from downstairs, the basement air
wet on my arms, cradling mushrooms
for the neighbors. Believe me, I am sung.

~

Feral as crows, there are children
pecking the stairs to splinters.
Once I'd have hidden in knotholes
making a snarl face. *So.*
With teeth I guard the home, and with breathing.
Here is our favorite bookshelf, overhead
is a plane going somewhere through clouds.
There was a rabbit who nested under
a good low shrub they took away
to make a smooth lawn; it hovered over babies,
quivering in an oval of bare dirt.

~

In the attic raw wood still bleeds
when the weather changes, nails protrude
from slanting beams. There are dolls
in a coffin bed, hands folded
over a crocheted blanket.
People learn to care about anything.
The lame field mouse dead in its makeshift cage
while cold air from a forgotten window

rubs recklessly against the furniture.

~

Bee hives create a line to measure.
So far from here to the next house, so far

to the sidewalk and pitted street. In the ravine
green streamers of ivy wrap the trees whose tops

are another horizon. Someone rides a bicycle
at sunset, becomes a calculation, darkness, circumscribed.

~

Tree trunks furred in moss, canopies
scattering pellets of light in the wet smoke
of the path. It has never not rained.
Below is a pasture with cows and fence.
Below that, white caps on the bay reflect
clouds, a bowl of shining discs.

~

Always there is something in the way. Dirt
or a patch that needs mending. It is hard
to be blind, to claw through the day.

~

The years are skeins of wildfowl
in flight, penning quick signatures the sky
erases before I'm half done looking.
At the river basin cranes come in fall,

spilling out of sight quick as the white sheets
of lightning that crack and flash in branches.

They are there, cacophonous on dark sand,

then not. Lifting, as they do, on one great
graceful wing of sound. In the aftermath

I am held still on my two heavy feet,
the trees arching over the clean shore
and the water I almost didn't see.

While I—breathless...

While I—breathless
with aching calves—
slogged among dunes
      two swift deer fell
and rose staggerless over sand
and lupine sown
back to life seed
by seed—what
were they doing
at bay—bared—fear
on their quick flanks
      if only eyes
wouldn't touch them
so and woods would
leap from gazes
and they into
that shaded sight
      a whale surfaced and then
another, a sleek phalanx,
those deer too, slick
salt spray and sweat
the shimmer light
keeps revealing—
      my feet
earthbound stones—
pulling as if
movement were such
simple wishing
dodging feathers
and all the shore's
beautiful dead
      strewn currency
for the taking
or the leaving
      and all to say
we can bury
or burrow—but

we will not be not seen
for long.

Self-Portrait with Uterine Fibroids

I was never winged, never half-
caste of horse and human, barely vengeful,
only I am marked by this distortion.
Honorary gash, it bleeds me

and so depleted,
I deform. I get so empty
I nearly drift

on air. I make a river to hold my place.
I am the river, running copper.
I've gone translucent

as the wing of a nymph,
an apparition.
My skin is paper; I mean
it is barely a cover, like a single onion skin,

the pale blue leaf of an aerogram.
Once on a street corner smiling at a neighbor
I nearly died. All the blood a body holds
can leak out quickly. I'd never been
so lightly tethered.

I wobbled, slanted quickly
toward the ground.
I was a girl engulfed in flame,

but now I'm spectral, misted stone.
I haunt cosmetic counters, pinch
my cheeks, offer wan assurances:
I'm fine I'm fine I'm hardly anywhere near dead.

Night Song

We are old and fall asleep
to the rattle of the hamster

making his rounds
on his squeaking wheel,

the shudder of cage vibrating
on the wooden table.

The house quivers until dawn
and I wake thinking about the baby crying,

how the sound of it used to saw
into my sleep, intertwine

so that I didn't so much wake
as will my dream into silence,

shaken finally by the signal—
more like an itch than a noise—

and sometimes I'd rouse
just one breath before the howl

as if my body knew,
a tremor sent through floor boards.

I was always so blurry, my breasts sore,
his little moody mouth pulling in and pushing away,

I worried I would damage him
with my secret, my desire to button my body back.

My love and fear and temper all ratted together
with unremembered threads of childhood.

And what if my poison leaked
into his organs or the insatiable hollows

his mouth was making in whatever once filled me?
Slow and clumsy, his body high on my shoulder

I navigated unlit rooms
untangling his fingers from their lock

on the wiry antennae of my tender scalp.

Wish

I want to lie down like a tiny birch canoe
sewn with red thread, afloat in the street,
in the rushing aftermath

of a good spring rain. To curl in the y of a desert willow
at sundown when its pink blossoms
are a thousand distant lanterns strung

among the branches. At night
I prop my tilted body like a shield.
I fly myself like a volley of arrows

toward the glowing eye of sleep's center.
I circle its edges, closing in. I call sleep's name
into closets and empty drawers and listen for its echo.

I want to lay my body into the palm
of my love's hand and diminish there,
a chip of ice. I want sleep to vanish me.

I'll lie curled in the dark
of the magician's hat, unhatched,
dreaming as my egg tooth sharpens.

Ghost Child of the Atalanta Bloom

This is what it's like to be the sun, hovering
above a rising and falling sheet
draped on the body on the mattress,
the body which is also my body
when I am not floating in the shadowless upper corner
of the room. To be the sun
is to be a swirling column of dust motes
the light has caught
and to be the light itself.
I was asleep and I was light.

~

In the morning wash of bright sun
the building's windows flare
and disappear alternately and a bird
wheels toward its own reflection,
wing tips brushing glass, leaving a visible arc,
a contrail on the retina
like a path one could follow to the next world.

~

In the dream in which there was light
and no light everything shone
as if polished, even the doorway
I knew would close, which was brightest
just before it closed and in those seconds I stole
my body back through in time
to catch my own steadying breath.

~

Each print pulled loose
from the suck of sand and water
follows the child as he runs

along the seam of shore
which the quick waves stitch and unstitch
to erase the evidence
of his passage.

~

We sat on the porch in the rain
after the bed ritual—the boy
talking to himself, making noises
as if he were bouncing nebulae off the ceiling
though we didn't usually check.
Gnats drowned in the wine
and we swallowed them. Guitar drifted across the street
and some low singing, bicycle tires and car lights sliding
over it all, the trees and the sound of trees
illuminated.

~

At the table, hands accordion matches
into tiny sculptures which litter the surface
like fallen sentries, statues
toppled at the entrance to an Etruscan tomb.
Eagle-headed god boys down on their knees.
Where the child's fingers
had been in the wax, a dozen little worlds
smoothed round and lined up
along the table's edge.
An iron-striped sunset in the window.

~

Imagine that some days even the grass
could be an engine of desire. The tassels which flash
in the wind so the whole field mirrors
the sugar running in your veins.

Your mouth a cloud of grainy words.
Maybe it happened this way.
The lover who used to whistle a song
to the cracked sidewalk—
you'd have known it anywhere.
The sound would cut through a wall of people
to reveal him, before you'd met, grinning in the dark.
He knew you by your ass, you knew him by his song.
The wind in the grass frenzies.
It was a trick of the moon,
this creation story.

~

Under the clouded sky
the ground glows as if lit from within.
A night like that.
The light like no light I knew.

ABOUT THE AUTHOR

Rebecca Aronson's first book, *Creature, Creature* won the Main-Traveled Press poetry contest and was published in 2007. She also received the 2010 Strousse Award from *Prairie Schooner*. Aronson's poems have appeared in *Tin House*, the *Georgia Review*, *Cream City Review*, *Mas Tequila Review*, *The Paris-American*, and *Quarterly West*, among other places. She lives in New Mexico where she teaches writing, facilitates a community writing group, and coordinates a visiting writers series for Central New Mexico Community College. She is co-curator of Bad Mouth, a series of words and music.

ABOUT ORISON BOOKS

Orison Books is a 501(c)3 non-profit literary press focused on the life of the spirit from a broad and inclusive range of perspectives. We seek to publish books of exceptional poetry, fiction, and non-fiction from perspectives spanning the spectrum of spiritual and religious thought, ethnicity, gender identity, and sexual orientation.

As a non-profit literary press, Orison Books depends on the support of donors. To find out more about our mission and our books, or to make a donation, please visit www.orisonbooks.com.